"It is as if we enhance our being if we can gain a place in the memory of others; it is a new life that we acquire, which becomes as precious to us as the one we received from Heaven."

- Montesquieu

Copyright 2020 Amarcord Journals

All rights reserved. No part of this publication may be reproduced, distributed or transmitted in any means without the prior written permission of the Publisher.

ISBN: 9798457219823

How to use this diary

◘ Read all the questions part of the different sections once in advance.

◘ For each question, try to elaborate your answer as much as you can within the available space.

◘ For "Story time" questions, take some time to reflect on your answers - sometimes memories need time to resurface.

◘ Once all questions and sections have been answered, write a special memo dedicated to your child in the space available at the start of the book.

Date: _____

My Dear _____

Family Origins

You

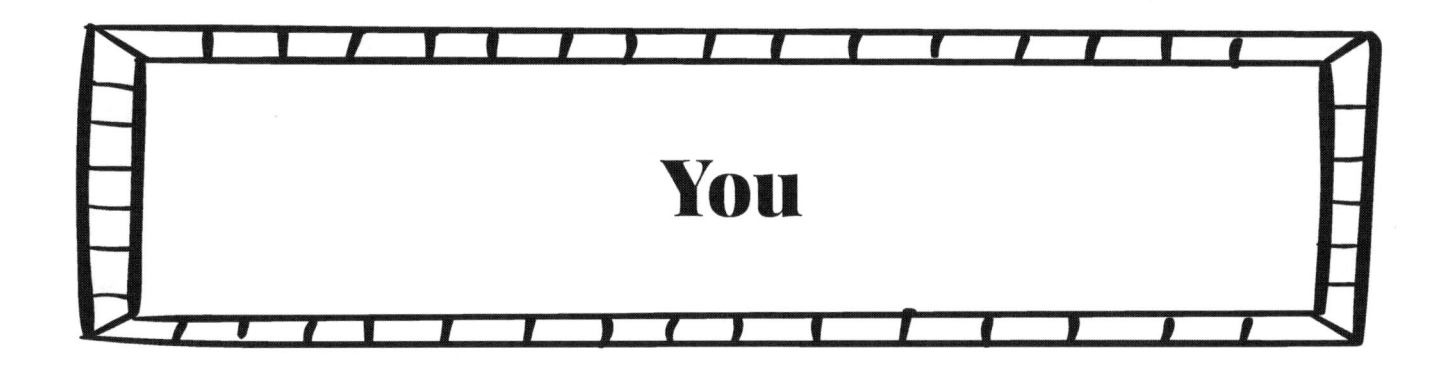

When and where were you born?

How did you get your name? Did you have a nickname?

_____
_____
_____
_____
_____
_____
_____
_____

Your Parents

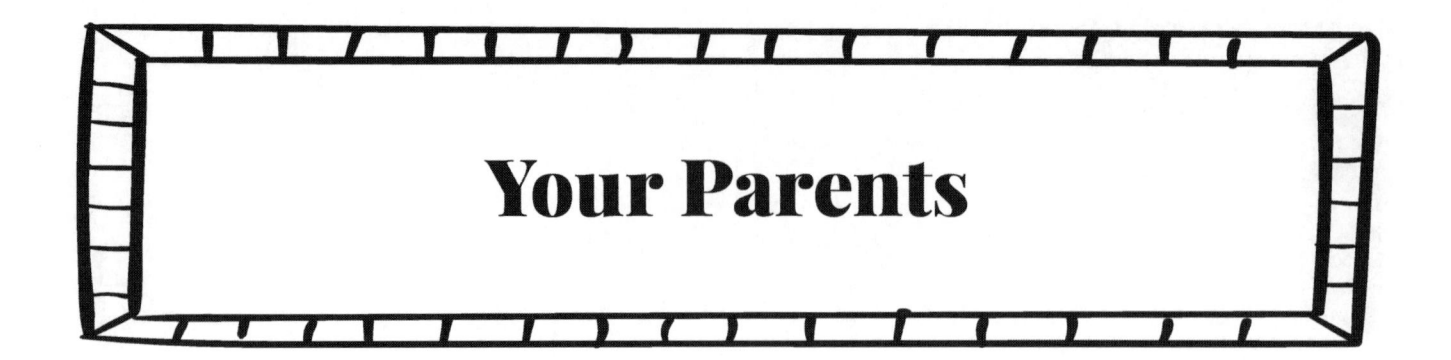

Tell me their names, birth dates and who they were

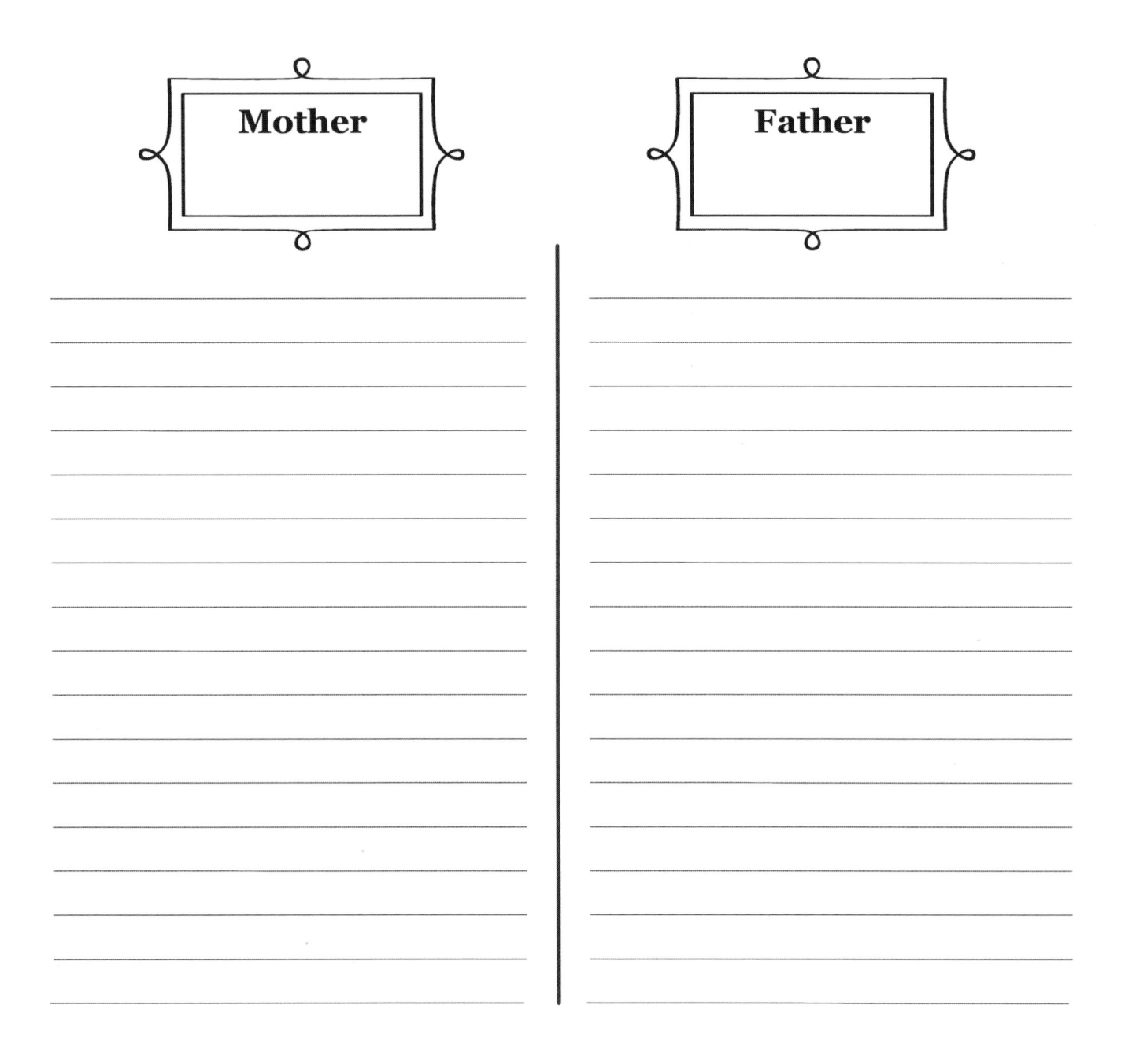

Mother	Father

How did your parents meet?

What kind of relationship did they have?

Story time

Write a most cherished memory of your mother

Story time

Write a most cherished memory of your father

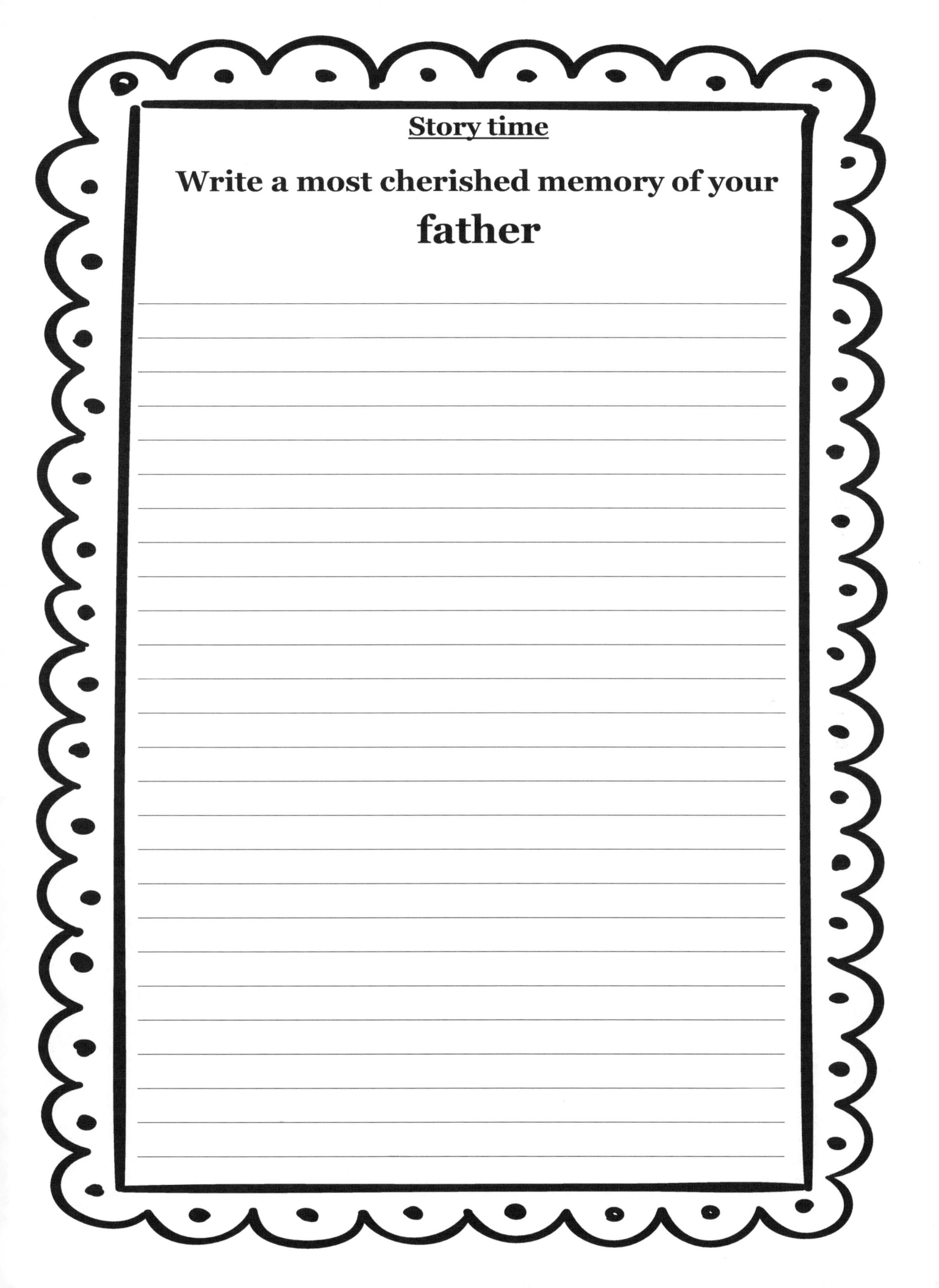

Siblings & Cousins

How many siblings did you have? List their names and year of birth:

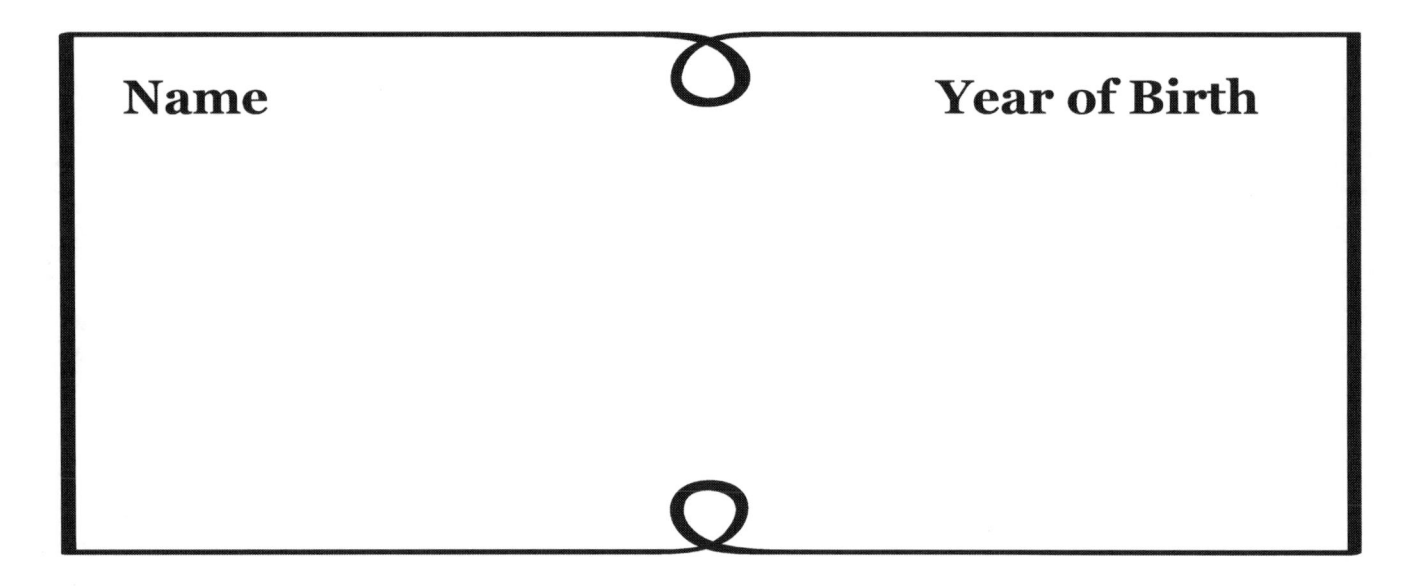

Name	Year of Birth

How was your relationship with them?

_____
_____
_____
_____
_____
_____
_____
_____

List all the names of cousins that you know of:

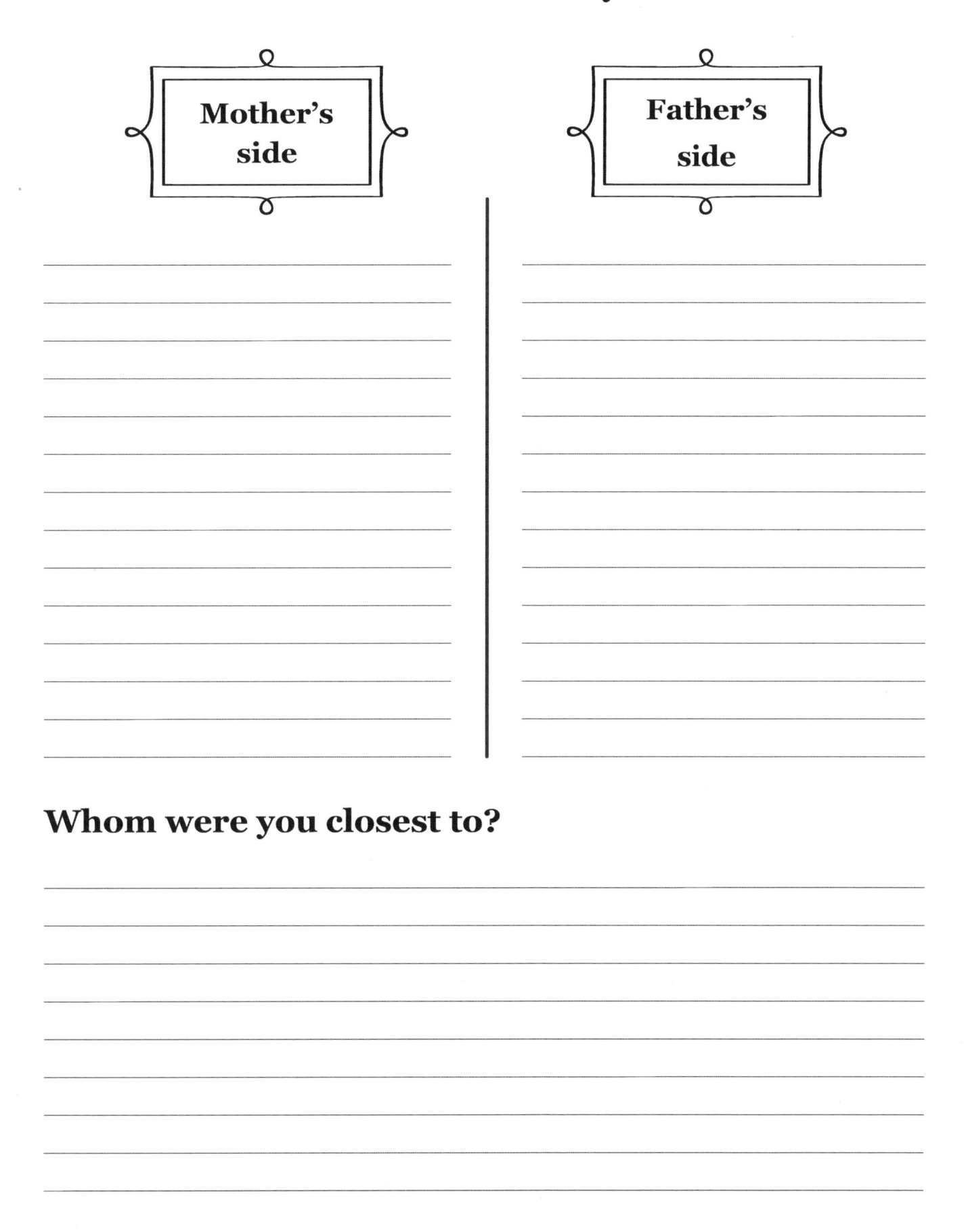

Mother's side	Father's side
_____	_____
_____	_____
_____	_____
_____	_____
_____	_____
_____	_____
_____	_____
_____	_____
_____	_____
_____	_____

Whom were you closest to?

_____
_____
_____
_____
_____
_____

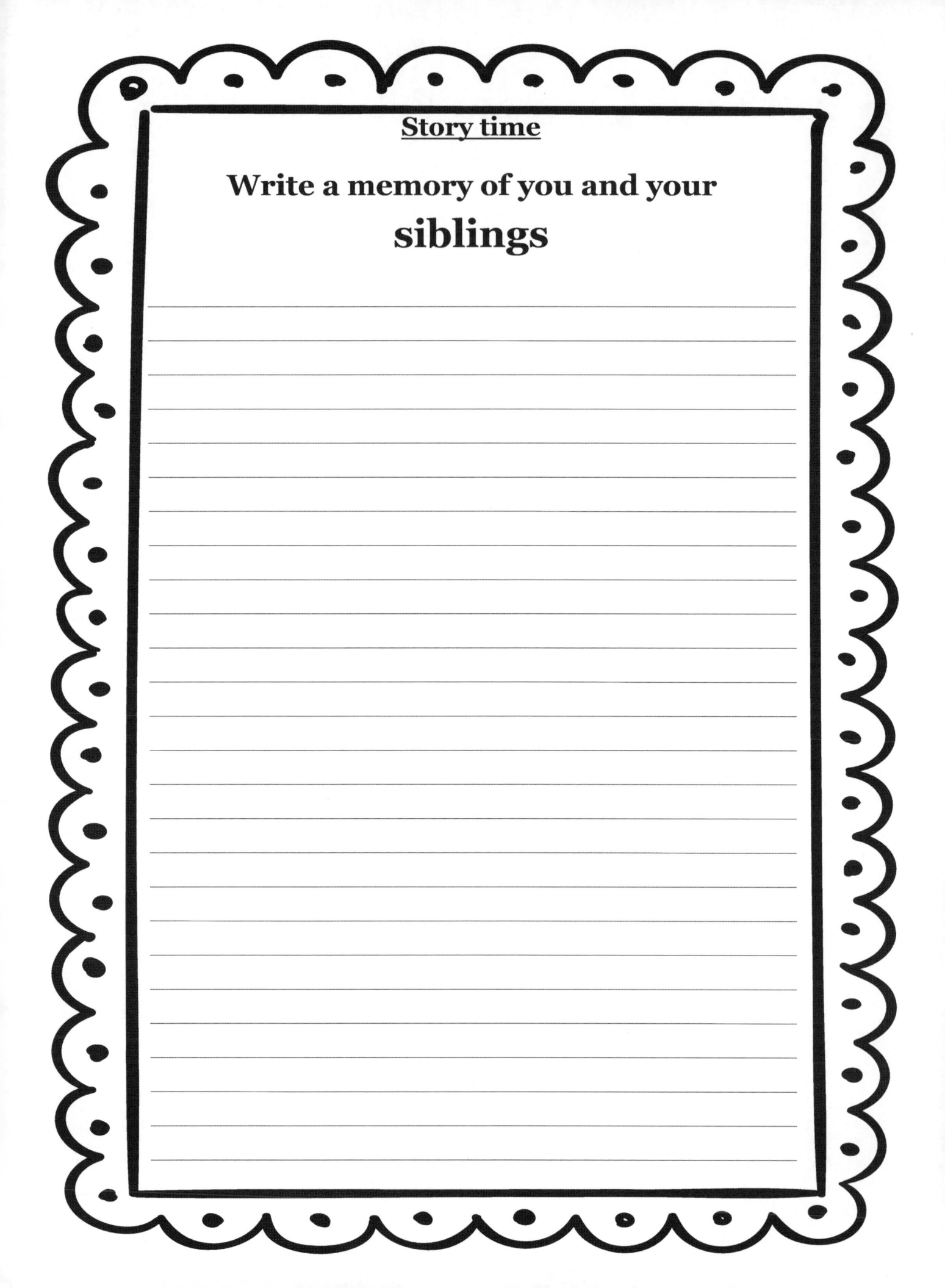

Story time

Write a memory of you and your **siblings**

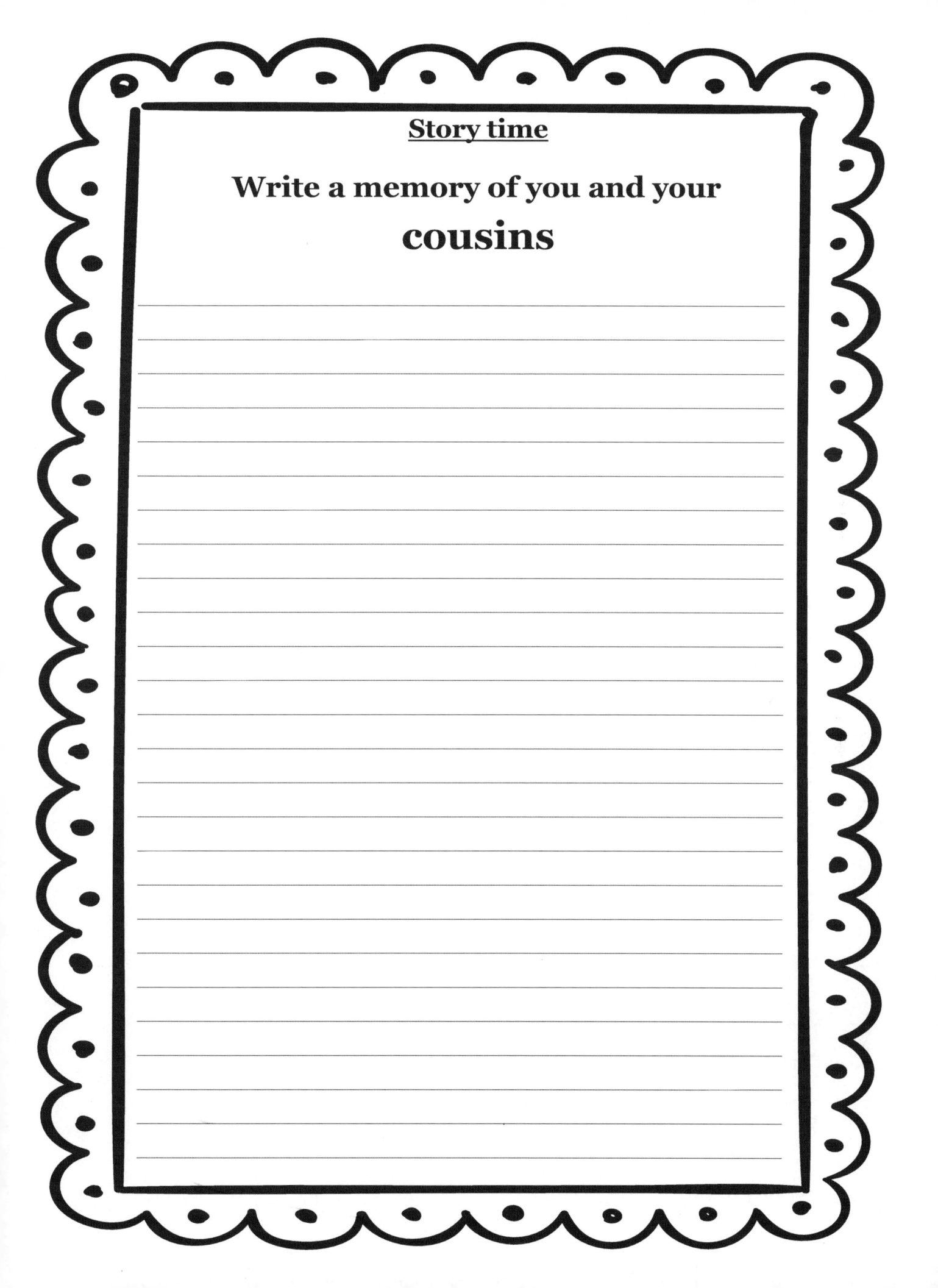

Story time

Write a memory of you and your **cousins**

The Wider Family

What are the regional and ethnic origins of our family?

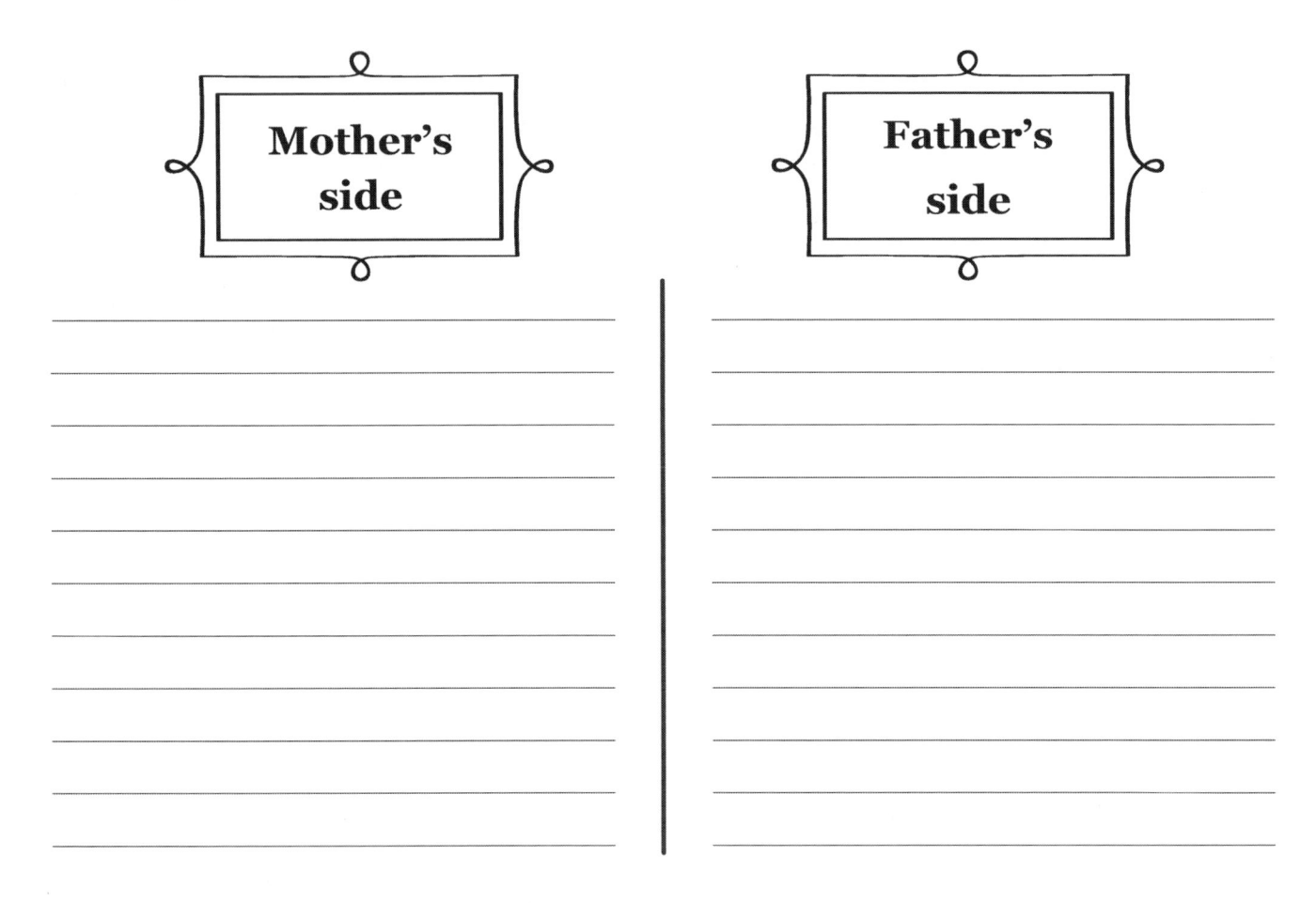

{ Mother's side }   { Father's side }

_____ | _____
_____ | _____
_____ | _____
_____ | _____
_____ | _____
_____ | _____
_____ | _____

Are there any recurring names?

What types of jobs and professions were common in the family?

Mother's side	Father's side
_____	_____
_____	_____
_____	_____
_____	_____
_____	_____
_____	_____
_____	_____
_____	_____
_____	_____
_____	_____

Were any of our ancestors well known for anything in particular?

_____
_____
_____
_____
_____
_____

Were there any object or properties that have been passed down from generation to generation?

Was there ever any feud or dramatic event in the family?

Story time

Write a cherished memory about your grandparents

How do you relate to your wider family and origins?

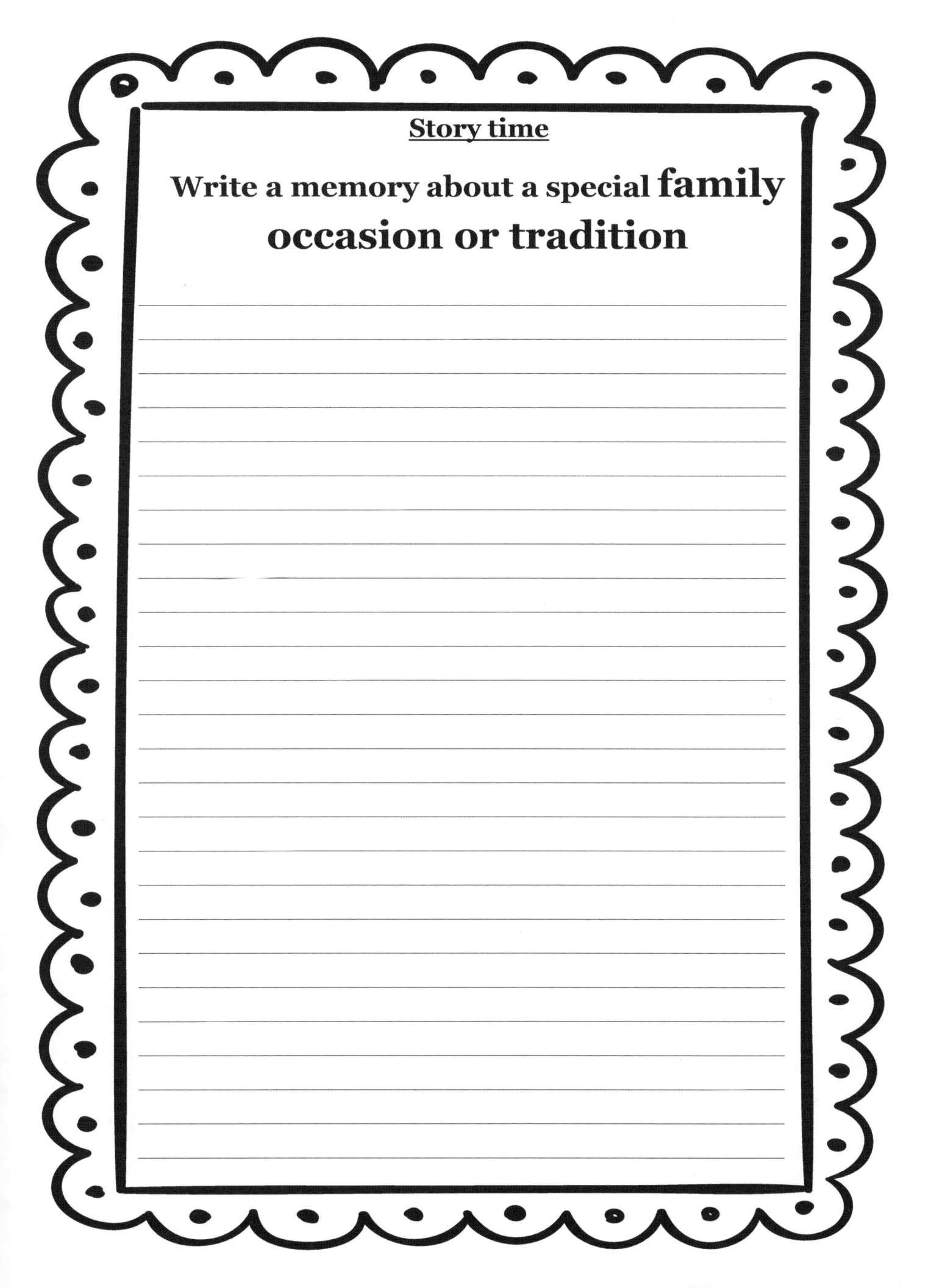

Story time

Write a memory about a special **family occasion or tradition**

How are you different from your parents and grandparents?

What is something you wish you had asked your parents but have not?

Childhood

Home & Family

What is your earliest memory as a child?

Where did you grow up? Tell me how was that place at that time

How was your childhood home? Describe the details you can remember of

---

Did you have a pet growing up?

Did you like animals in general?

Were you close to your parents as a kid?

How were you as a child? Were you difficult or well behaved?

Story time

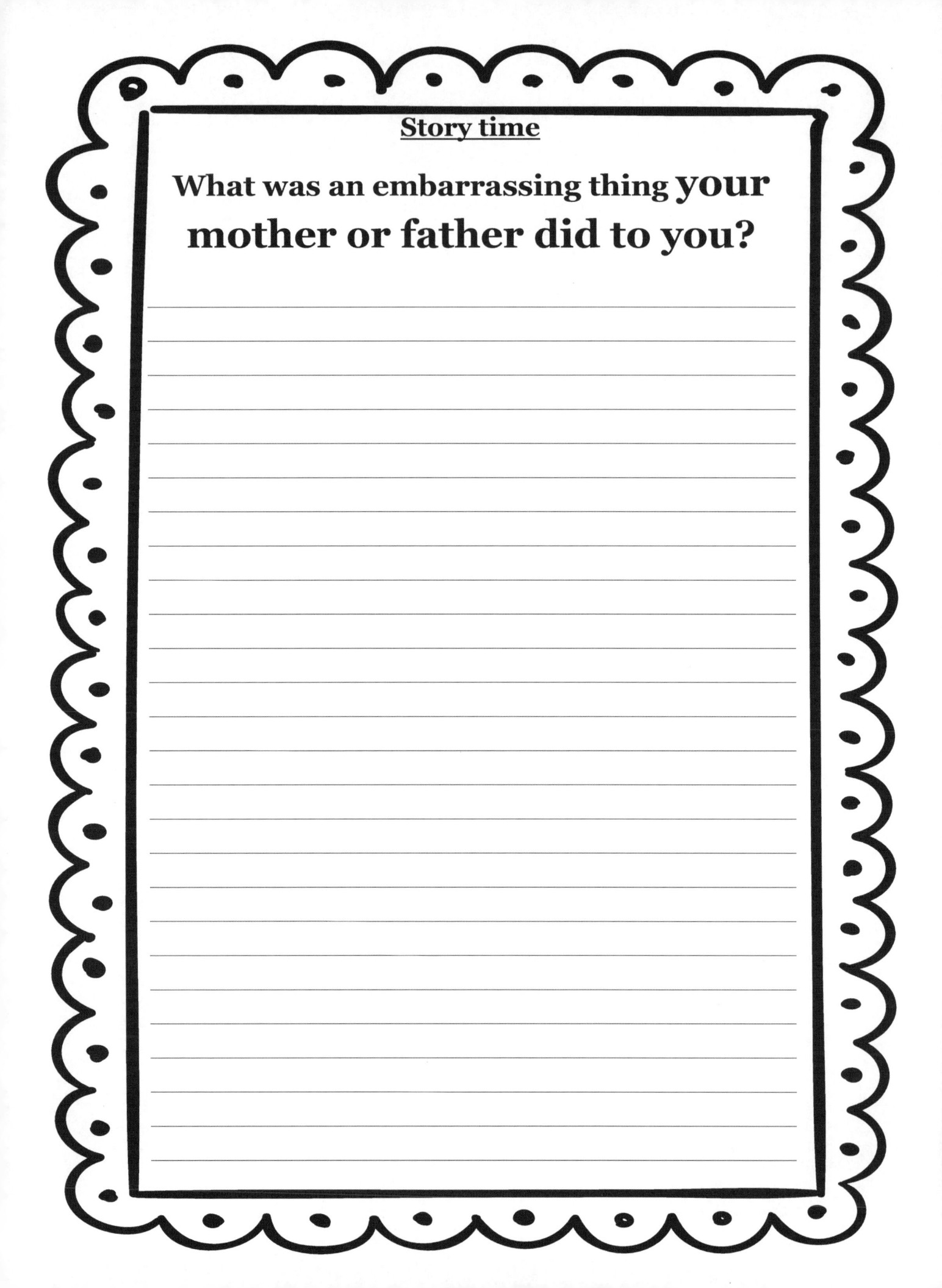

What was an embarrassing thing your mother or father did to you?

What's one thing your parents always used to tell you growing up that turned out to be true?

Friends & School

Who were your best friends during childhood?

Names

What games would you play together?

Story time

Write a memory about one of your childhood friends

Did you enjoy going to school?

| **What did you wear at school?** | **What kind of things and supplies did you use in class?** |

How was going to school in those days compared to nowadays?

Life as a Child

Describe a typical day in your life as a kid:

How did you spend Christmas and other festivities with your family?

How and where would you normally spend the summer holidays?

Story time

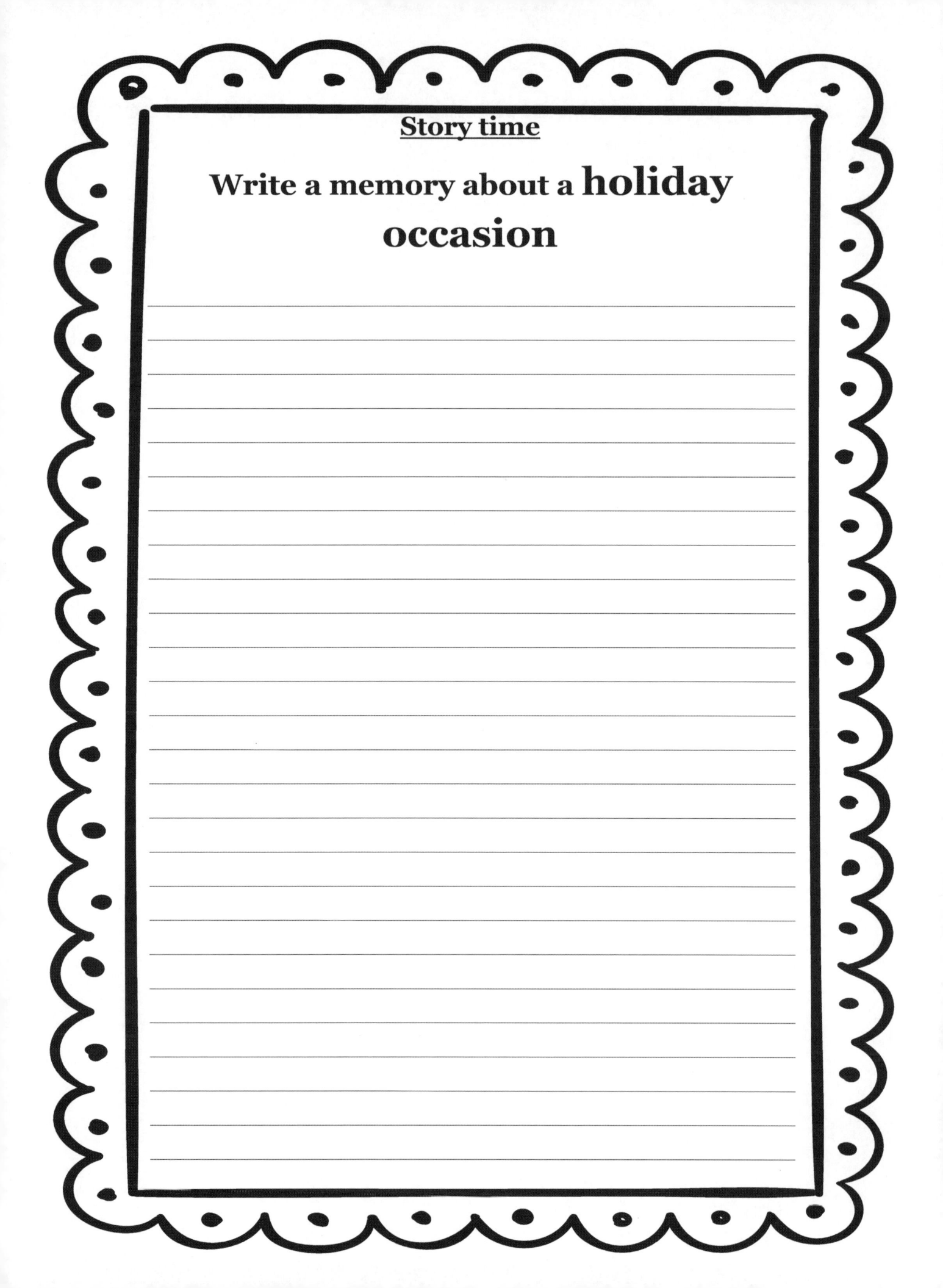

Write a memory about a **holiday occasion**

_____
_____
_____
_____
_____
_____
_____
_____
_____
_____
_____
_____
_____
_____
_____
_____
_____
_____
_____
_____
_____
_____
_____

Story time

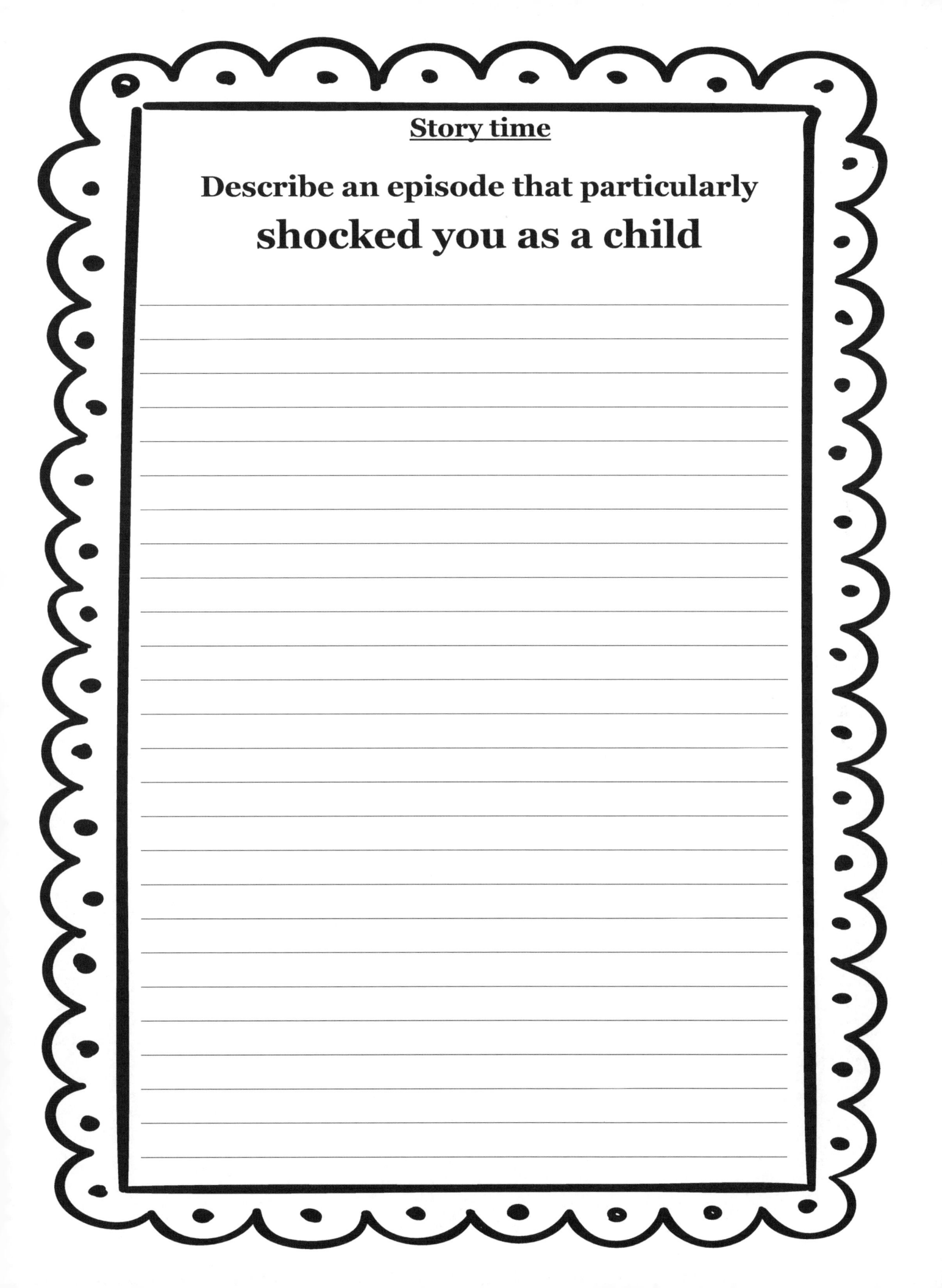

Describe an episode that particularly shocked you as a child

What was an early talent you had as a child?

Who was a role model for you?

Story time

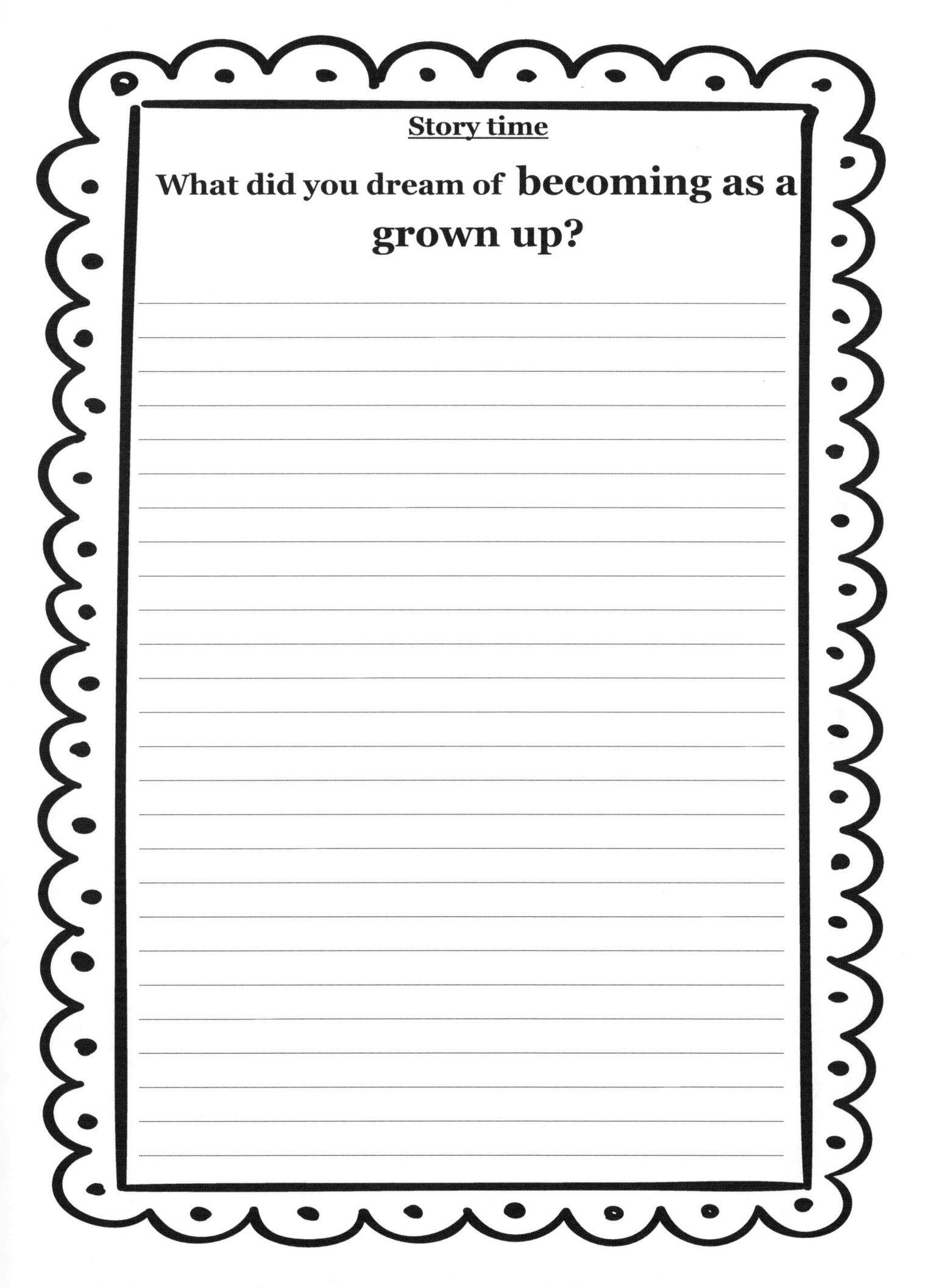

What did you dream of becoming as a grown up?

Teens

School & Leisure

Where did you attend secondary and high school?

Were you a good pupil?

Do your remember any of your teachers? Was there any of them that motivated you in particular?

| What were your favourite subjects? | And your least favourite subjects? |

How would you usually spend your time outside of school?

Were you part of any clubs or did you have any hobbies?

What kind of music did you like?

Did you play any instrument?

Or wanted to learn to play any instrument?

When did you first drive a car and how did you learn to drive?

Relationships

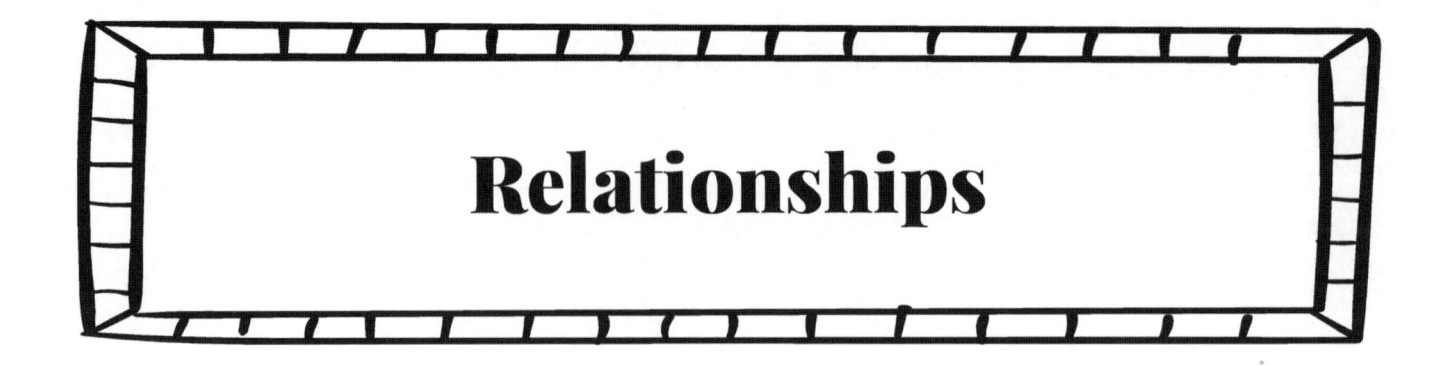

Did you get along with your parents? How was your relationship with them as a teenager?

Who was your best friend?

How did you normally spend time together?

Did you keep in touch over the years?

How did young boys and girls interact in those days?

Did you have a special friend from the opposite sex?

Story time

Write your memories about your **first crush**

Life as a Teenager

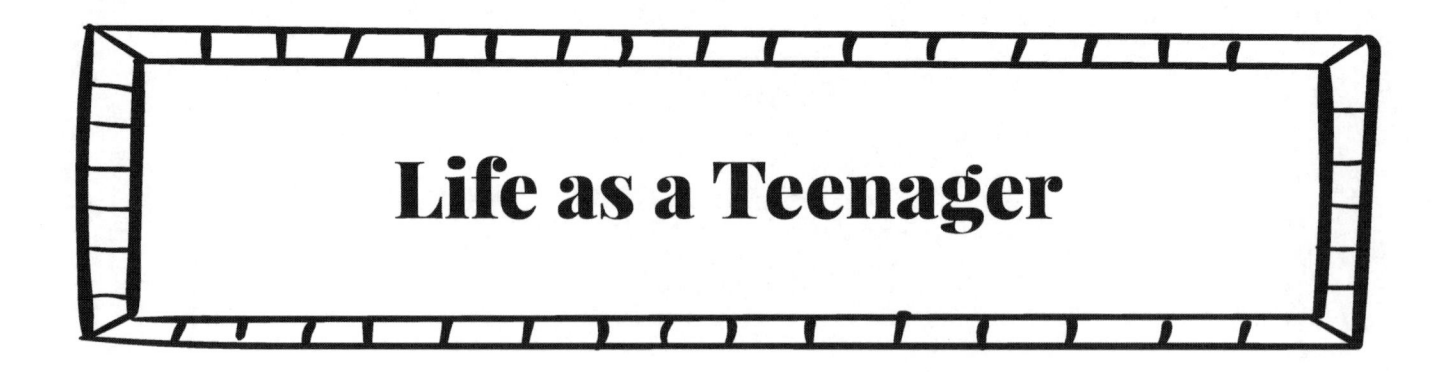

What kind of personality did you have as a teenager? Were you more outgoing or introvert?

Did you enjoy being a teenager?

Who did you look up to?

What did you want to do after graduating?

Story time

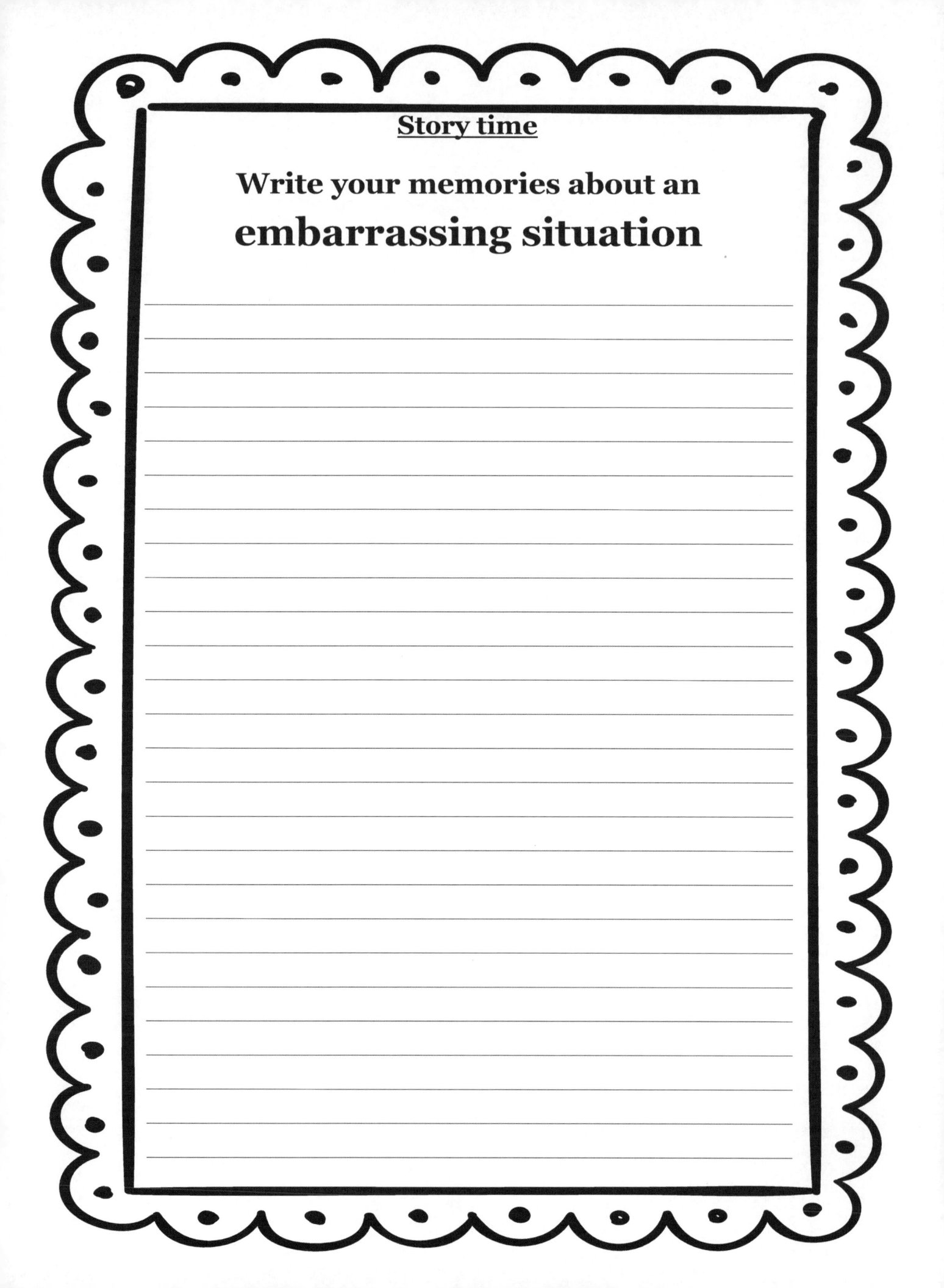

Write your memories about an embarrassing situation

What are the differences and commonalities about being a teenager in those days and nowadays?

What do you miss about those years?

Adulthood

Work & Career

Did you go to complete higher education? How did you gain your professional skills?

What was your profession and how did you get into it?

What was your favourite job?   **What was your least favourite job?**

What would have been a profession you would have liked to pursue?

_____
_____
_____
_____
_____
_____

How do you feel about retirement?

_____
_____
_____
_____
_____
_____

Life as a Grown-up

Where was your first adult home?

Story time

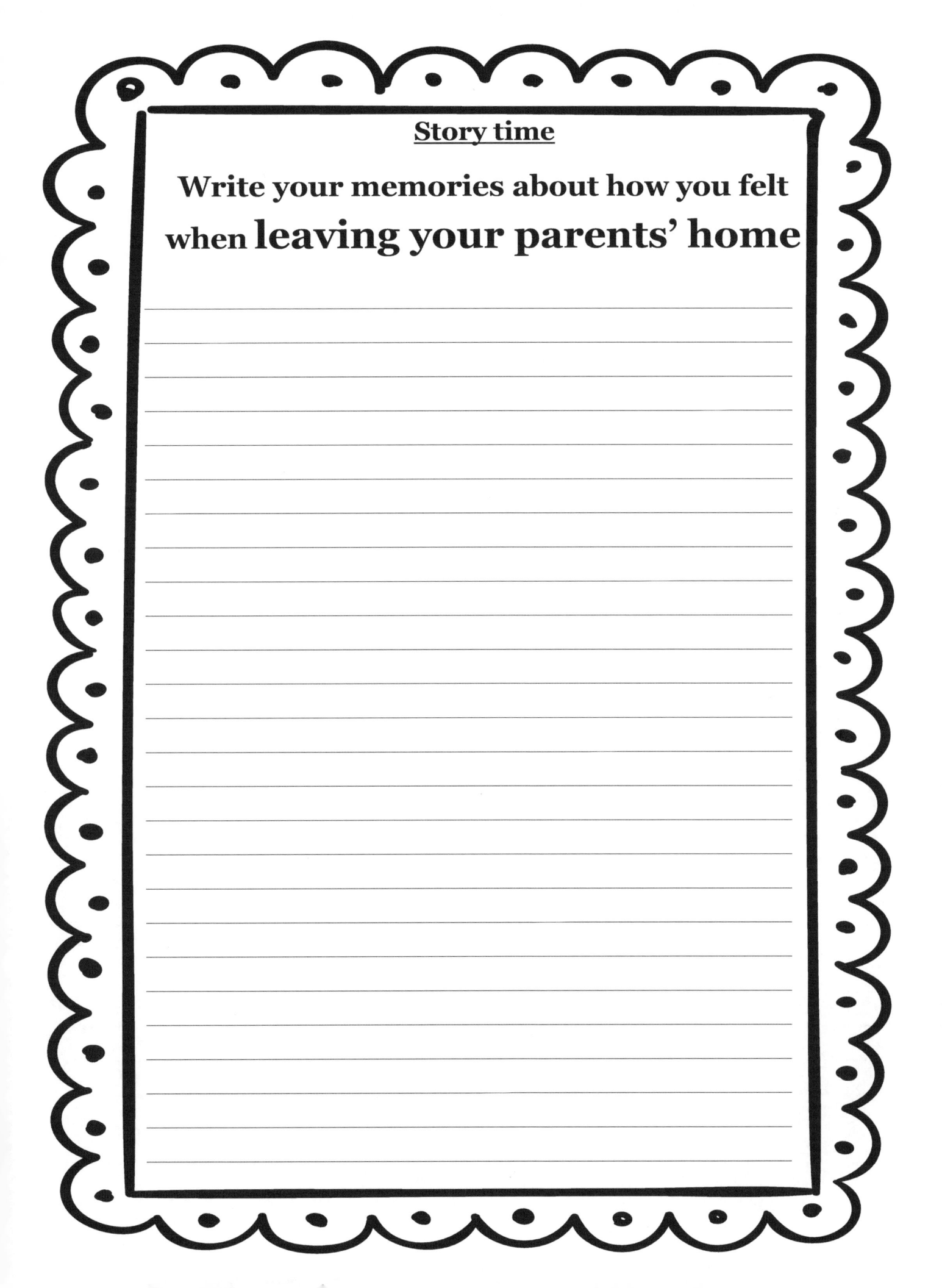

Write your memories about how you felt when leaving your parents' home

Did you live in the same place during your adult life or did you move around?

Where is your favourite place in the world?

Story time

Write about a memorable trip

Love & Relationships

Who was the first person you said "I love you" to in a romantic context?

How did you first meet dad?

How did you understand you had fallen in love and that it was the right person for you?

Story time

Write your memories about the first date with dad

When did your relationship become official?

| What things did you like most about him? | What things did you like least? |

How did love evolve over time for you?

Do you have any regrets when it comes to love?

Story time

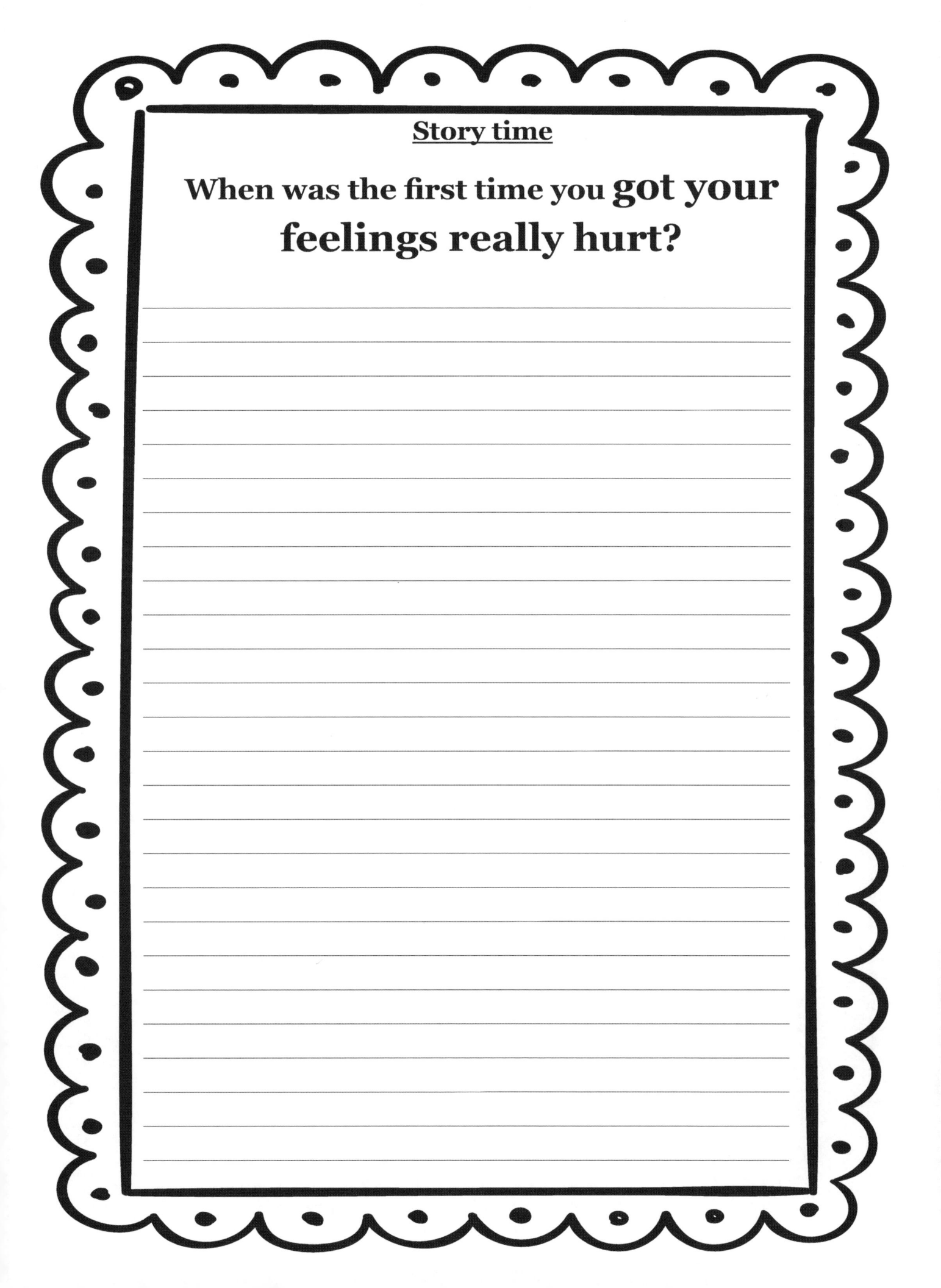

When was the first time you got your feelings really hurt?

Who have been the most important friends throughout your life?

What are the qualities that have made relationships meaningful for you?

Story time

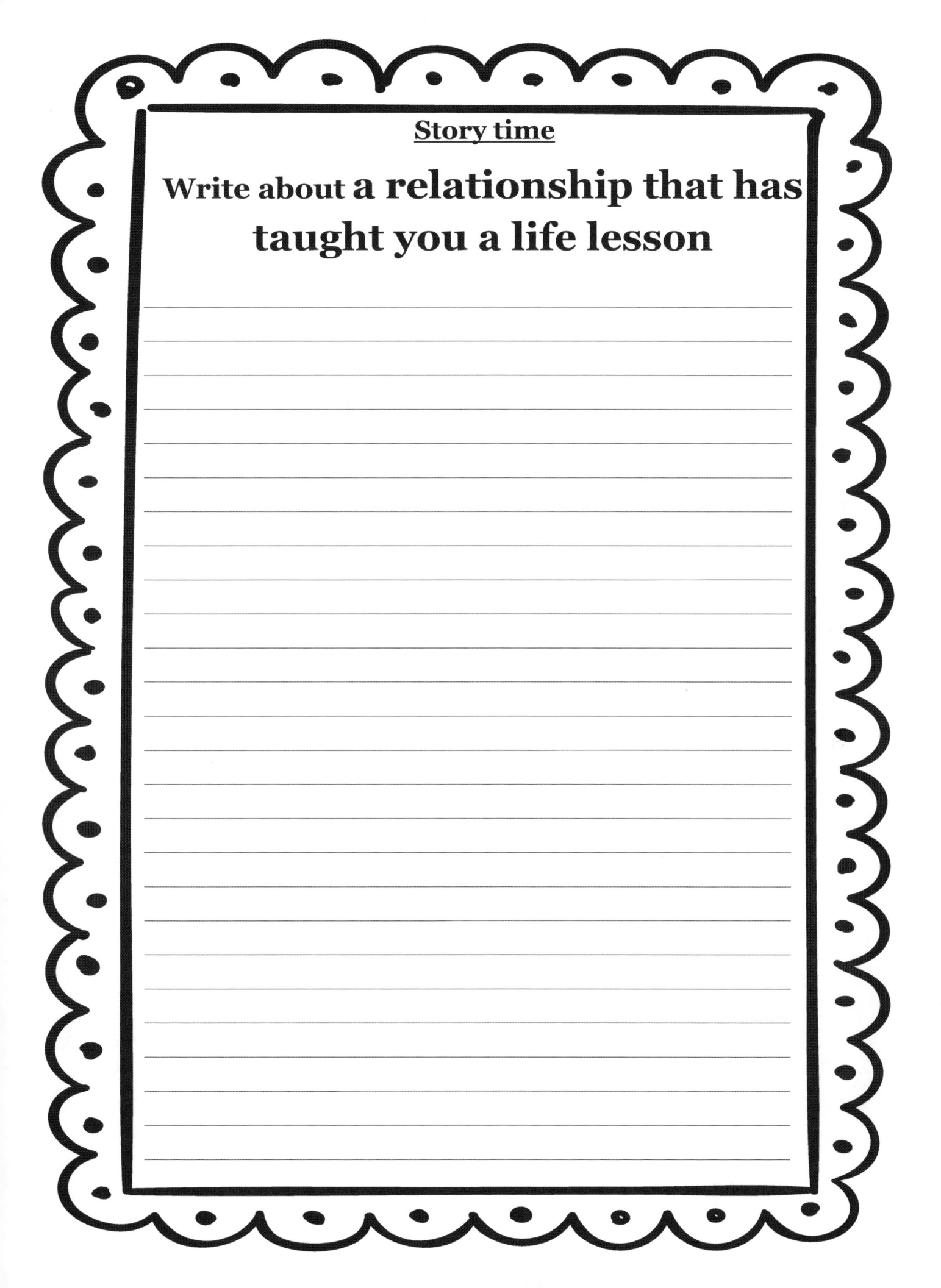

Write about **a relationship that has taught you a life lesson**

Parenthood

Becoming a Mum

How old were you when you first became a mother?

Did you always want to have a family?

_____
_____
_____
_____
_____
_____
_____
_____
_____
_____
_____
_____
_____
_____
_____
_____
_____

How did you find out you were going to become a parent?

Were you hoping to have a son or a daughter?

How did you pick names? What other names were considered?

What did you apprehend most about becoming a parent?

Story time

Write your memories about **the first days after I was born**

Raising Kids

Was parenting easier or harder than you expected?

Did you have any support to care for your children?

What things did you enjoy most as a parent?

And what things did you enjoy the least?

Story time

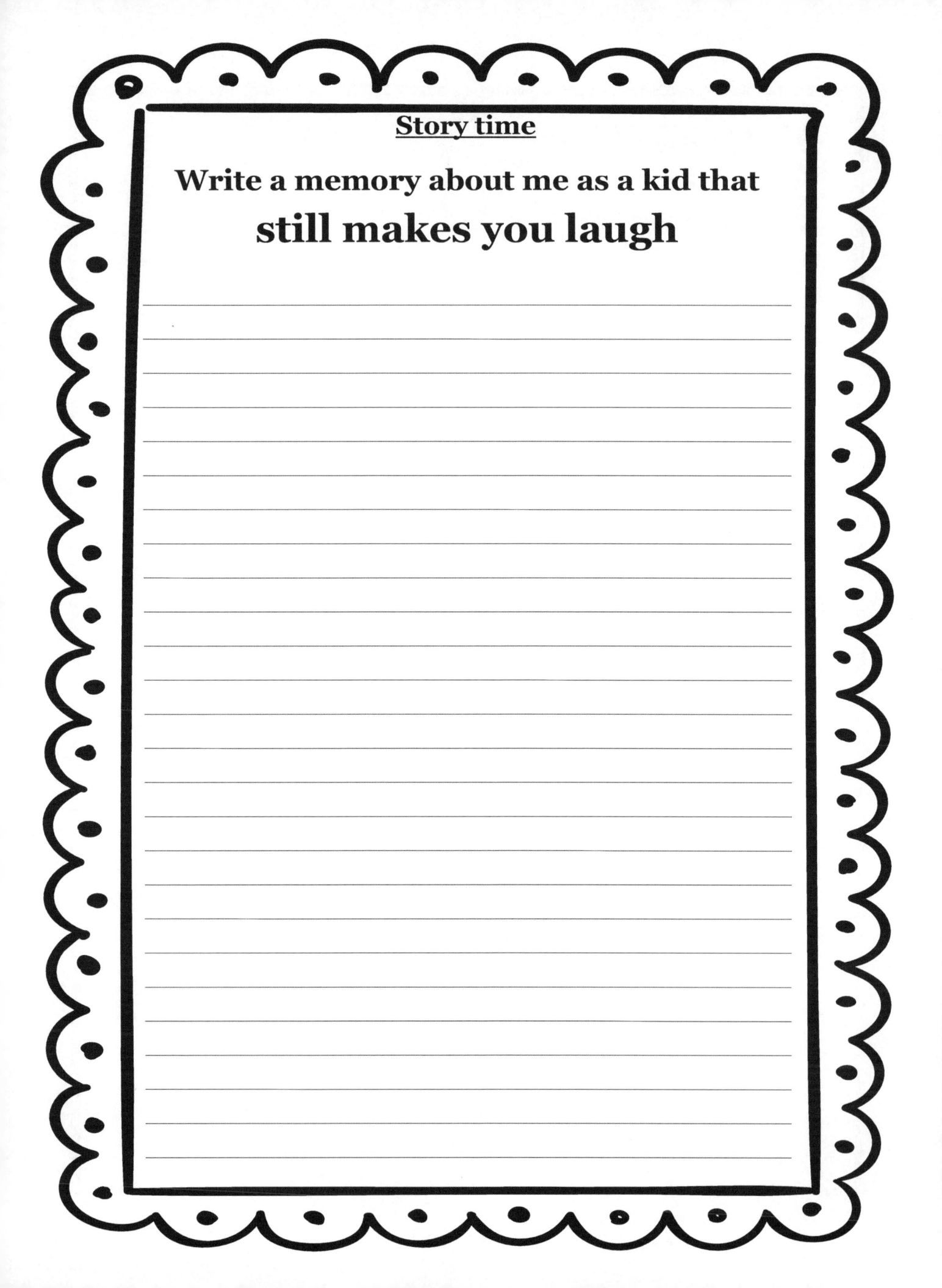

Write a memory about me as a kid that still makes you laugh

What aspect of yourself do you see in me?

What character traits are different between us?

Being a Parent

How did you choose your parenting style?

How do you see yourself as a parent compared to other parents you know?

What was the biggest challenge for you as a parent?

If you could go back and change anything about being a parent, what would you do differently?

How did you evolve as a parent?

What is somethings that you learned by being a parent?

Present Time

Looking Back

What has been your favourite age so far and why?

What are you most proud of in your life?

What is one of your biggest regrets in life?

What have been your biggest fears?

Is there something you've always wanted to do, but never got the chance?

How has your idea of what it means to be a woman changed over the span of your life?

Pearls of Wisdom

What are your biggest hopes for your children and grandchildren?

What is your best advice on how to make good choices?

What is your best advice on friendship?

What is your best advice for a successful loving relationship?

What is your best advice on how to be a parent?

What is your best advice on how to be successful in life?

What is your best advice on how to be happy in life?

Is there anything else you would want to tell me?

Printed in Great Britain
by Amazon

64b86191-ada3-4f43-a7fd-7fa89cd45edbR01